Highlights

Hidden Pictures

AWESOME SCIENCE PUZZLES

HIGHLIGHTS PRESS

Honesdale, Pennsylvania

Welcome, Hidden Pictures Puzzlers!

When you finish a puzzle, check it off √. Good luck, and happy puzzling!

Contents

☐ Lab-radors at Work 4–5

☐ Geology Class..................... 6

☐ Wild Wind........................ 7

☐ An Active Arbor Day............. 8

☐ Solar System Studies 9

☐ Photosynthesizing Friends...... 10

☐ Aurora Borealis 11

☐ Science Fair Fun............... 12–13

☐ Night Lights...................... 14

☐ Kitchen Chemistry............... 15

☐ Wonderful Waterfall 16

☐ Habitat Cleanup 17

☐ Bunny Paleontologists........... 18

☐ Ocean Exploration 19

☐ Ready for Takeoff!............... 20

☐ Wildlife Portrait.................. 21

☐ How Old Are These Trees?...... 22

☐ Balancing on Waves 23

☐ Robot Lab 24–25

☐ Alpine Air......................... 26

☐ Bat Habitat 27

☐ Exciting Experiment 28

☐ Water in Winter.................. 29

☐ Dinosaur Display................. 30

☐ Butterfly Hike 31

☐ Cave Wave 32–33

☐ Great Geyser! 34

☐ Jungle Inspection 35

☐ Large Charge 36

☐ Ocean Ecosystem 37

☐ Desert Discoveries 38–39

☐ Pond Pals........................ 40

☐ Eye on the Sky................... 41

☐ Ants Up Close................ 42–43

☐ Moose Tracks 44

☐ Space Explorers 45

☐ Culinary Experiments........... 46

☐ Where Are the Birds?............ 47

☐ Treetop Physics............... 48–49

☐ Penguin Posing 50

☐ Skeletons, Big and Small 51

☐ Spreading the Compost......... 52

☐ Antarctic Adventurers 53

☐ A Day at the Museum....... 54–55

☐ Out in Space 56

☐ Hermit Habitat................... 57

☐ Sparkling Science 58

☐ Will the Boat Float?.............. 59

☐ Coral Curiosity 60–61

☐ Physics in Action 62

☐ Dormant Volcano Tour........... 63

☐ Veterinary Care 64

☐ Outdoor Expedition.............. 65

☐ What Can You See? 66–67

☐ Aquatic Environment 68

☐ School Garden................... 69

Cover art by James Lancett

Pretend Doctor 70

Spectacular Spelunking 71

What Weather! 72

Bzz-y Bees 73

Rocket Ship Repairs......... 74–75

Gurgling Geyser 76

A Trip to the Zoo 77

Rockin' Binoculars............... 78

Ready, Set, Grow!................. 79

Feeding the Seals 80

Dino Dig 81

Robo Baker.................. 82–83

How Much Rain?................. 84

Look at Them Grow! 85

Science Class.................... 86

Beach Observations............. 87

Snowshoe Scientists 88–89

Dinosaur Museum 90

Science Fair Creations 91

Bayou Biology 92

Wind and Waves 93

Telescope Time.................. 94

Robot Building................... 95

A Whale of a Time 96–97

Feeding Fish 98

Science Rules!................... 99

Hi There, Heron! 100

Rock Candy Crystals........... 101

Deep-Sea Submarine 102–103

Microscopic Marvels 104

Geology Rocks 105

Exploring the Lake 106

Low-Gravity Games............. 107

Computer Lab 108–109

Collecting Samples............. 110

Careful Assembly Required..... 111

Family Zoo Day............. 112–113

Space Dreams 114

Nature Center Visit............. 115

Terrific Tyrannosaur 116–117

Soundwaves in the Sky 118

Who's in the Tide Pool? 119

Observant Eyes................. 120

Water Cycle Workshop......... 121

Immersive Oceanography...... 122

Hey, Comet! 123

Defying Gravity 124

Topographic Trek............... 125

Community Garden........ 126–127

Objects in Motion 128

Build-Your-Own Catapult....... 129

Answers.................... 130–144

Lab-radors at Work

ice-cream cone

worm

magnet

candle

comb

light bulb

loaf of bread

flashlight

bucket

flowerpot

toothbrush

mushroom

mug

domino

ladder

diamond

boot

feather

golf tee

mallet

butter knife

bean

barbell

button

flag

screw

Art by Mary Sullivan

5

Geology Class

pushpin

pencil

snake

button

banana

Art by Brian Michael Weaver

hockey stick

ring

cotton swab

fishhook

seashell

adhesive bandage

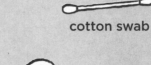
horseshoe

teacup

6

Wild Wind

closed umbrella

crescent moon

bowl

drinking straw

pointy hat

pennant

fried egg

tea bag

candy corn

artist's brush

table-tennis paddle

scarf

screw

jump rope

top hat

stick of gum

Art by Scot Ritchie

7

An Active Arbor Day

Art by Paula Becker

flashlight

artist's brush

envelope

crown

wedge of lemon

heart

slice of pizza

ruler

crescent moon

fried egg

needle

mitten

8

Solar System Studies

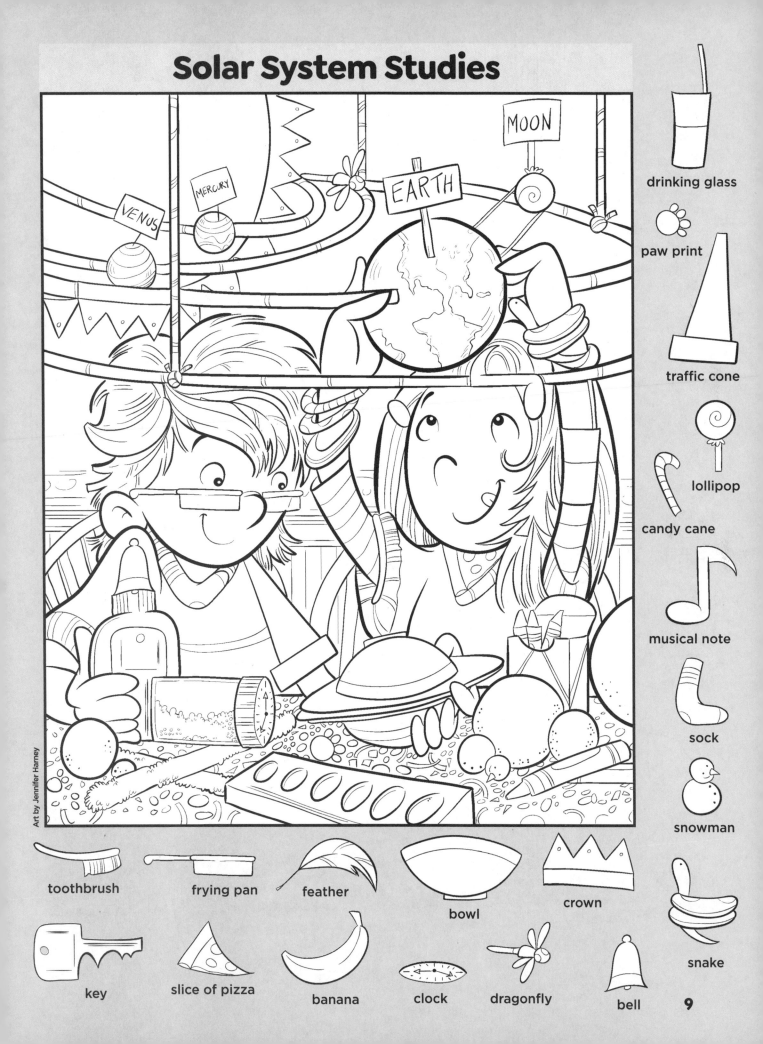

Photosynthesizing Friends

lightning bolt

toothbrush

sailboat

suitcase

fish

comb

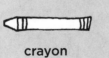

crayon

teacup

arrowhead

crab

crown

pine tree

slice of pie

banana

duck

10

Art by Sonya Montenegro

Aurora Borealis

banana

fish

crown

bow tie

boot

candle

drinking straw

feather

fork

ice-cream bar

cat

arrow

spoon

muffin

sock

Art by David Sheldon

11

Science Fair Fun

golf club

drinking straw

lollipop

umbrella

bell

iron

crown

flute

hammer

four-leaf
clover

nail

key

leaf

glove

paw print

bucket

VINEGAR

BAKING SODA
VINEGAR
CO2

VOLCANO

12

mallet

pencil

musical note

ladder

sailboat

grapes

mushroom

banana

hat

ring

button

party horn

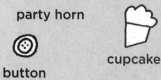
cupcake

crescent moon

open book

earmuffs

Art by Laura Close

Night Lights

can

magnifying glass

clock

light bulb

glove

fork

watering can

ice-cream cone

apple

banana

airplane

button

wedge of orange

candy cane

spoon

ruler

crown

envelope

Art by Héctor Borlasca

Kitchen Chemistry

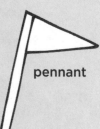
banana

candle

shuttlecock

shoe

cowbell

dart

sock

slice of pie

mushroom

toothbrush

arrowhead

ring

ladder

car

pennant

Art by Mary Sullivan

15

Wonderful Waterfall

 cotton candy

 boomerang

 apple

stool

 pickle

acorn

beehive

 lamp

 hot dog

 football

muffin

 caterpillar

mitten

tea bag

Habitat Cleanup

grapes

lemon

teardrop

loaf of bread

golf club

baseball bat

pennant

hat

ring

tadpole

needle

snake

pencil

ruler

sailboat

key

pickax

eyeglasses

artist's brush

chopsticks

Art by Laura Close

17

Bunny Paleontologists

musical note

book

slice of bread

flag

teacup

mitten

envelope

duck

key

spoon

crayon

comb

pencil

ruler

saltshaker

toothbrush

Art by Mike DeSantis

18

Ocean Exploration

teacup

glove

bell

flower

boomerang

ring

eyeglasses

banana

goose

elf's hat

sailboat

hat

nail

owl

Art by Tim Davis

Ready for Takeoff!

sailboat

kite

spool of thread

baseball bat

ruler

yo-yo

pencil

crown

ring

envelope

tack

candle

banana

bell

slice of pie

Art by David Helton

20

Wildlife Portrait

paper clip

candle

hamburger

glove

slice of pie

spoon

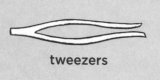
tweezers

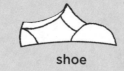
shoe

heart

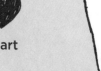
ice-cream cone

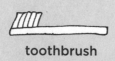
toothbrush

banana

crown

Art by Tim Davis

21

How Old Are These Trees?

slice of pizza

sock

doughnut

ring

butter knife

wedge of cheese

potato

ice-cream bar

Art by Mike Moran

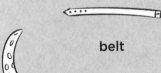
belt

crown

seashell

crescent moon

pennant

rolling pin

pencil

22

Balancing on Waves

cane

golf club

crescent moon

flag

artist's brush

cotton candy

question mark

nail

slice of pie

needle

bird

heart

party hat

toothbrush

fishhook

Art by Sally Springer

23

Robot Lab

drumstick

hockey stick

ladder

lollipop

drinking straw

ring

mug

adhesive bandage

saltshaker

envelope

worm

game piece

megaphone

sailboat

cane

question
mark

plunger

key

crescent
moon

comb

wedge of
lemon

acorn

cinnamon bun

slice of
pizza

ruler

Art by Patrick Girouard

25

Alpine Air

ax

sailboat

mitten

sock

drinking glass

nail

candle

ice-cream cone

spoon

carrot

cupcake

book

boot

handbag

snake

Bat Habitat

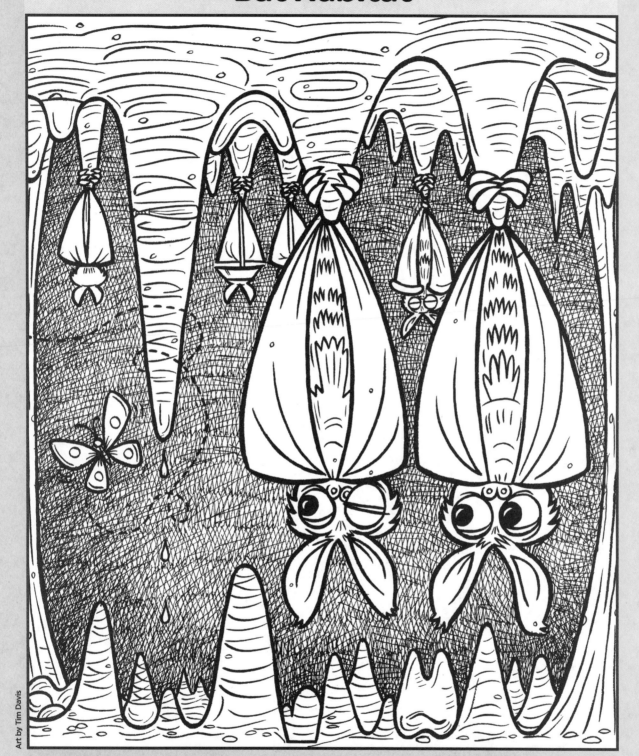

mitten

elf's hat

bell

ice-cream cone

glove

tooth

bird

boomerang

sailboat

paper clip

teacup

banana

fish

baseball bat

Exciting Experiment

SCIENCE FAIR

JUDGE

ghost

canoe

ruler

needle

hockey stick

ax

candle

cookie

magic wand

artist's brush

boomerang

carrot

fish

leaf

teacup

banana

magnet

crescent moon

crown

bell

olive

sock

envelope

doughnut

snake

Water in Winter

Art by Mike Moran

potato

seashell

magnet

balloon

stamp

domino

wedge of
orange

flashlight

ruler

flag

slice of pizza

snake

envelope

ice-cream cone

Dinosaur Display

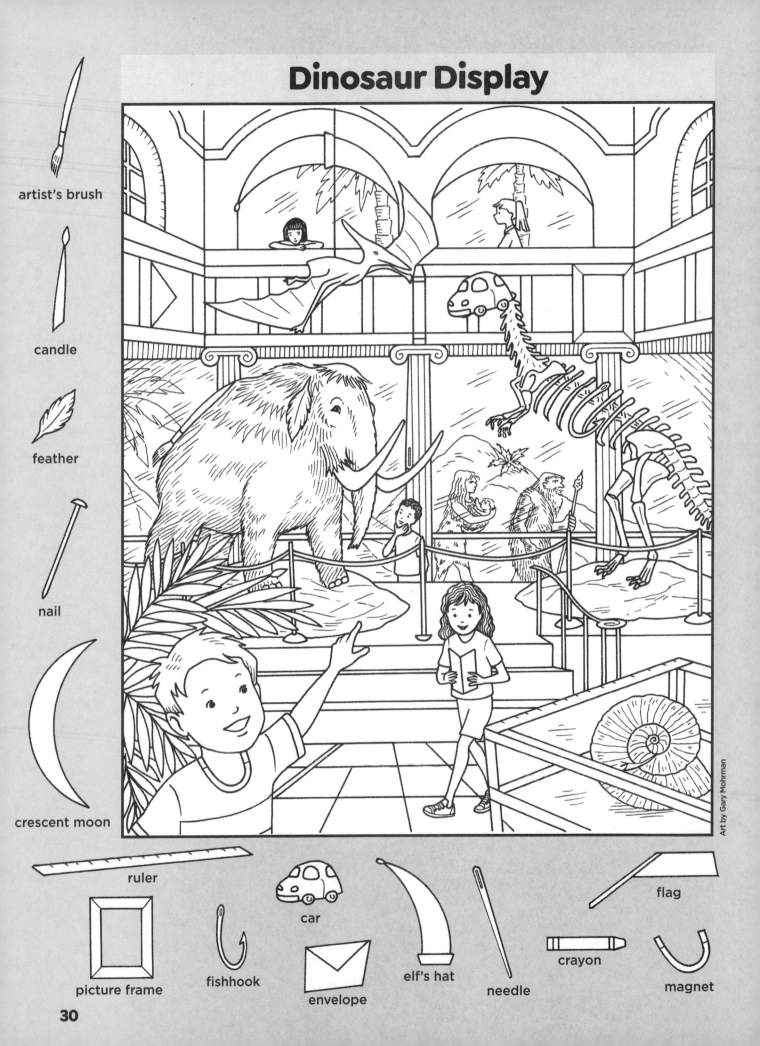

artist's brush

candle

feather

nail

crescent moon

ruler

picture frame

fishhook

car

envelope

elf's hat

needle

crayon

flag

magnet

Art by Gary Mohrman

Butterfly Hike

shovel

wishbone

scissors

ring

lock

seashell

ice-cream cone

lemon

artist's brush

scrub brush

pencil

mitten

canoe

computer mouse

spoon

mug

crown

Art by Ron Lieser

31

Cave Wave

sock

button

envelope

spoon

wristwatch

flashlight

ladle

kite

golf club

drinking glass

marshmallow

mug

ice-cream cone

Art by David Helton

Great Geyser!

heart

skateboard

pear

star

pencil

needle

trowel

crescent moon

horseshoe

slice of pie

rabbit

duck

candle

whistle

hat

Jungle Inspection

chili pepper

pennant

scissors

heart

spoon

golf tee

peapod

high-heeled shoe

slice of pie

crayon

bottle

iron

ice-cream bar

flag

ring

flowerpot

arrow

35

Art by Gary Mohrman

Large Charge

fish

comb

sock

cane

feather

bowling pin

bird

duck

ruler

baseball bat

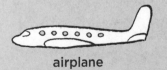
airplane

rabbit

Art by Rob Shepperson

Ocean Ecosystem

baseball bat

vase

baseball

button

carrot

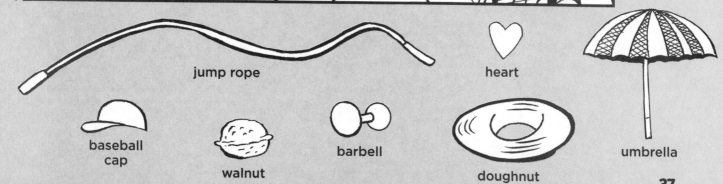

jump rope

heart

umbrella

baseball cap

walnut

barbell

doughnut

37

Desert Discoveries

adhesive
bandage

balloon

candle

tooth

crescent
moon

crown

fried egg

fishing
pole

pig

golf club

flowerpot

funnel

green bean

heart

high-heeled
shoe

teacup

mitten

dog bone

snowflake

wishbone

closed
umbrella

needle

lightning
bolt

wedge of
orange

pineapple

saucepan

saltshaker

pickle

piece of
popcorn

rolling pin

toothbrush

matchstick

Art by Laura Close

39

Pond Pals

toothbrush

necktie

carrot

artist's brush

ice-cream cone

closed umbrella

40

fork

ice-cream bar

candy cane

plate

baseball bat

scissors

ring

glove

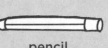
slice of pie

pencil

peanut

Art by Lyn Martin

Eye on the Sky

sailboat

key

boot

needle

flashlight

duck

wedge of lemon

slice of pie

bird

mushroom

pennant

toothbrush

acorn

ruler

Art by Jim Bertram

41

Ants Up Close

fan

bell

matchstick

elf's shoe

slice of pie

eyeglasses

closed umbrella

lightning bolt

crescent moon

bow tie

sailboat

crown

42

teacup

party hat

heart

balloon

iron

snowman

arrow

paper airplane

fish

boomerang

Art by Laura Close

43

Moose Tracks

hat

deer

sailboat

spoon

coat hanger

feather

banana

bird

duck

heart

fish

butterfly

44

Art by Tim Davis

Space Explorers

drinking
straw

fishhook

teacup

button

needle

cane

lollipop

game
piece

caterpillar

hat

pencil

iron

musical
note

ice-cream
bar

mallet

Art by Laura Close

Culinary Experiments

heart

rabbit

T-shirt

bowling pin

light bulb

top hat

key

feather

slice of pizza

46

ring

eyeglasses

hammer

safety pin

baseball cap

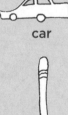
car

toothbrush

whale

spool of thread

crescent moon

pine tree

hockey stick

Where Are the Birds?

Art by Mary Sullivan

butter knife

teacup

mallet

pencil

sock

fishhook

rowboat

flute

slice of pizza

banana

toothbrush

game piece

party hat

golf club

muffin

pennant

Treetop Physics

fork

crown

flower

cactus

brush

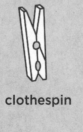
clothespin

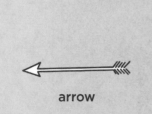
arrow

saw

feather

screwdriver

48

high-heeled
shoe

glove

game piece

dog bone

pine tree

crescent
moon

coat hanger

knitted hat

alligator

crutch

closed umbrella

slice of pizza

Art by Iryna Bodnaruk

Penguin Posing

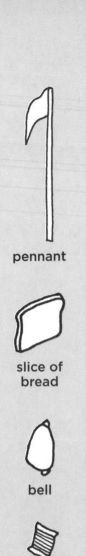
pennant

slice of
bread

bell

spool of
thread

musical
note

party horn

drumstick

Art by Laura Close

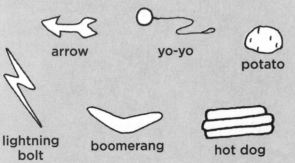
arrow

yo-yo

potato

lightning
bolt

boomerang

hot dog

mushroom

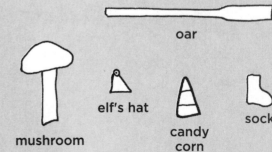
oar

elf's hat

candy
corn

sock

50

Skeletons, Big and Small

Art by Brian Michael Weaver

teacup

banana

spool of thread

lollipop

feather

piece of popcorn

envelope

domino

bell

toothbrush

telescope

sock

hockey stick

ring

snake

mallet

bowling ball

paintbrush

Spreading the Compost

golf club

comb

teacup

cane

heart

pencil

slice of pizza

candle

domino

ring

fork

envelope

drinking straw

ruler

artist's brush

52

Art by Mitch Mortimer

Antarctic Adventurers

rabbit

ice-cream cone

battery

boomerang

candle

baseball bat

key

flower

saw

pencil

shoe

comb

slice of pizza

sneaker

banana

spoon

toothbrush

saucepan

hairbrush

eyeglasses

ruler

cheeseburger

pickle

sock

Art by Travis Foster

A Day at the Museum

muffin

bugle

shoe

fishhook

pencil

rake

baseball bat

mitten

slice of bread

football

paper clip

rooster

chili pepper

umbrella

sailboat

Art by Kevin Rechin

roller skate

house

spoon

bell

flashlight

flashlight

slice of pie

Out in Space

screwdriver

horn

pencil

ring

mug

candle

needle

crescent moon

toothbrush

light bulb

heart

bell

shoe

banana

sailboat

hat

book

Hermit Habitat

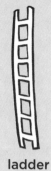
ladder

slice of pizza

comb

barbell

glove

candle

fishhook

heart

candy corn

pine tree

wedge of lime

lightning bolt

canoe

worm

bottle of glue

piece of popcorn

caterpillar

sailboat

Art by Kevin Zimmer

57

Sparkling Science

needle

feather duster

envelope

adhesive bandage

carrot

piece of popcorn

58

boomerang

seagull

screw

hockey stick

mitten

artist's brush

Art by Brian Michael Weaver

Will the Boat Float?

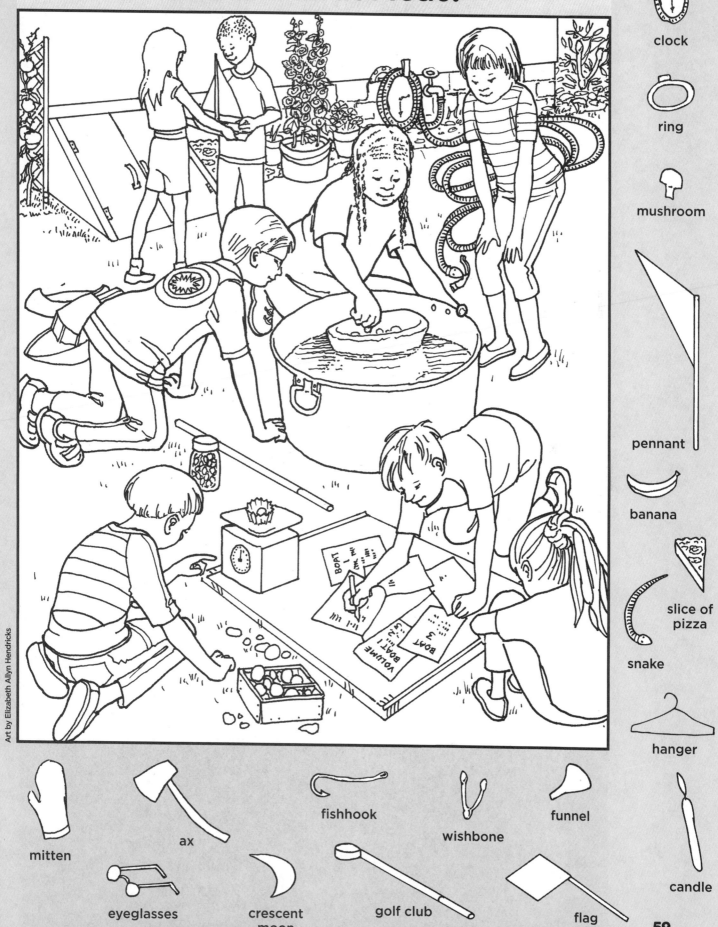

clock

ring

mushroom

pennant

banana

slice of pizza

snake

hanger

mitten

ax

fishhook

wishbone

funnel

eyeglasses

crescent moon

golf club

flag

candle

Art by Elizabeth Allyn Hendricks

Coral Curiosity

fishhook

glove

spoon

banana

clothespin

cane

ring

wishbone

fork

nail

key

wedge of cheese

heart

ice-cream cone

teacup

tack

goblet

candle

needle

Art by Sally Springer

mitten

crescent moon

slice of bread

crayon

button

slice of pizza

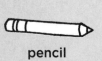
pencil

baseball cap

61

Physics in Action

lightning bolt

cane

nail

mitten

hairbrush

shovel

pennant

musical note

slice of pizza

heart

horseshoe

wedge of orange

pickle

crown

pie

Art by Laura Close

62

Dormant Volcano Tour

beet

cupcake

crescent moon

teacup

ruler

frog

envelope

bird

crown

banana

toothbrush

snake

sailboat

slice of pizza

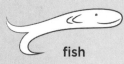
fish

Veterinary Care

vacuum

valentine

vase

vest

vine

violin

viper

volcano

vegetable

volleyball

Art by Mattia Cerato

64

Outdoor Expedition

gingerbread cookie

snail

slice of pie

bowling pin

penguin

green bean

paintbrush

cupcake

pitcher

plunger

canoe

hot dog

toothbrush

dinosaur

carrot

Art by Chuck Dillon

65

What Can You See?

chicken hawk

turkey vulture

snowy owl

goldfinch

hummingbird

chickadee

nuthatch

snow goose

Carolina wren

red-tailed hawk

osprey

kite

HAWK MOUNTAIN COUNTER

66

great horned owl

goshawk

grosbeak

Canada goose

woodpecker

cardinal

mourning dove

blue jay

harrier hawk

golden eagle

bald eagle

Art by Linda Weller

67

Aequatic Environment

baseball bat

tweezers

spoon

banana

cupcake

house

paper clip

slice of pizza

slice of pie

vase

mushroom

heart

slice of bread

baseball cap

sock

open book

Art by Maggie Swanson

68

School Garden

lollipop

cane

boot

elf's hat

artist's brush

ice-cream cone

slice of pie

stick of gum

loaf of bread

drinking glass

seashell

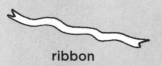
ribbon

fish

staple

canoe

Art by Gary Mohrman

69

Pretend Doctor

cookie

seashell

shovel

slice of cake

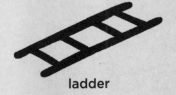
ladder

hammer

slice of pizza

fried egg

Art by Kelly Kennedy

Spectacular Spelunking

snake

adhesive bandage

glove

button

crescent moon

carrot

pushpin

sock

bowling pin

teacup

ruler

artist's brush

comb

ice-cream cone

envelope

potato

yo-yo

pencil

ice-cream bar

slice of pizza

frying pan

Art by Brian Michael Weaver

What Weather!

ice-cream bar

bowl

paper airplane

fishhook

flag

balloon

pennant

ruler

lollipop

sailboat

toothbrush

heart

trowel

spatula

horn

sheep

slice of cake

UMBRELLA STORE

UMBRELLAS

NEWS

Bzz-y Bees

teacup

bell

cupcake

canoe

saucepan

boomerang

feather

fork

cauldron

frying pan

dog dish

slice of pie

kite

dog bone

slice of pizza

rocket ship

pen

pennant

artist's brush

tack

wishbone

trowel

derby hat

sailboat

butter knife

spoon

Rocket Ship Repairs

pencil

ring

caterpillar

baseball
bat

lollipop

book

key

sock

slice of pizza

tack

teacup

comb

banana

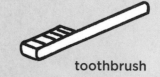
toothbrush

Art by R. Michael Palan

75

envelope

ice-cream
bar

comb

tack

lollipop

mushroom

candle

football

Gurgling Geyser

spoon

party hat

boot

balloon

adhesive
bandage

artist's brush

canoe

kite

A Trip to the Zoo

ELEPHA

head

ea

trunk

tusk

pencil

adhesive bandage

zipper

screw

artist's brush

diamond

heart

shovel

worm

apple

spoon

snail

mitten

cookie

slice of pizza

comb

baseball

pair of pants

duck

snow cone

sailboat

Art by Jennifer Harney

Rockin' Binoculars

crescent moon

funnel

slice of cake

banana

golf club

caterpillar

lima bean

hockey stick

heart

drinking straw

teacup

envelope

tweezers

ice-cream cone

NATURE CENTER

NATURE TRAIL ▷

Art by Ron Lieser

Ready, Set, Grow!

paper airplane

game piece

hot dog

musical note

crescent moon

ladder

baseball bat

adhesive bandage

ruler

wedge of lemon

pencil

croquet mallet

pizza

pennant

can

fish

Art by Dana Regan

79

Feeding the Seals

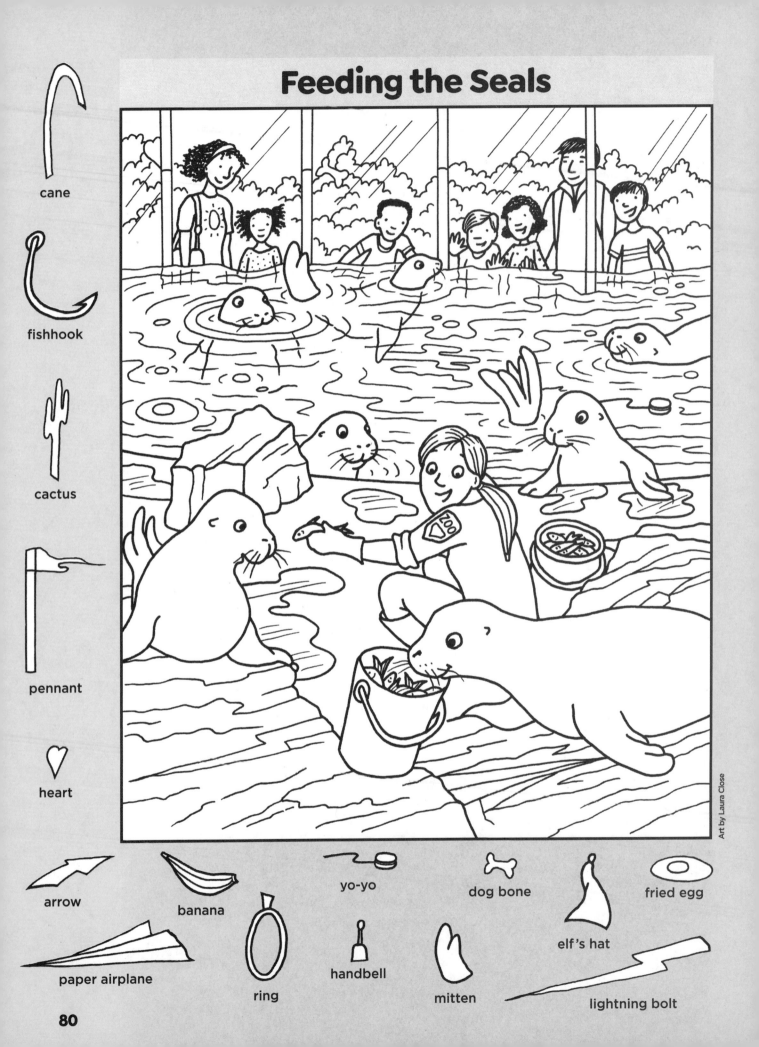

cane

fishhook

cactus

pennant

heart

arrow

banana

yo-yo

dog bone

fried egg

paper airplane

ring

handbell

mitten

elf's hat

lightning bolt

Art by Laura Close

80

Dino Dig

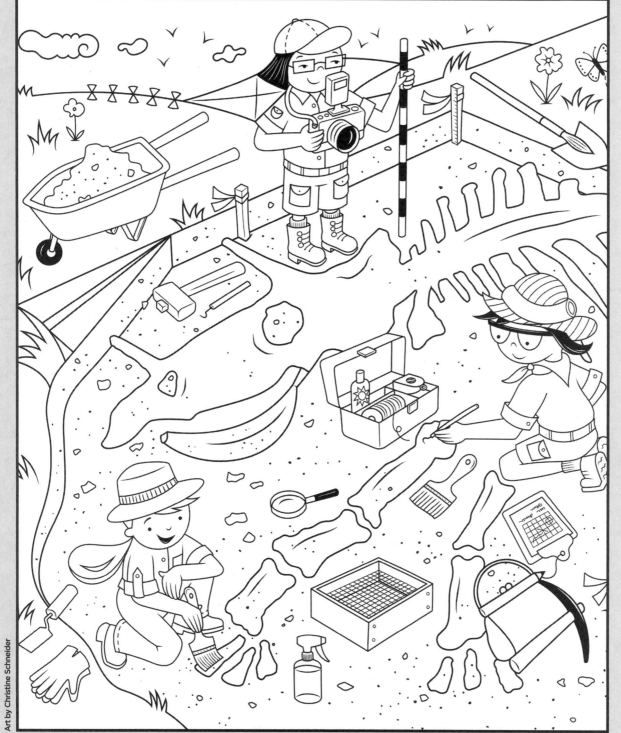

elbow noodle

kite

artist's brush

teardrop

banana

ruler

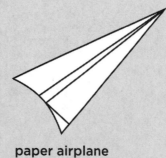
paper airplane

handbag

Art by Christine Schneider

81

Robo Baker

bottle

chef's hat

button

glove

drinking straw

ax

baseball bat

canoe

comb

slice of pizza

feather

slice of cheese

pretzel

heart

hat

coat hanger

toothbrush

vase

envelope

crescent moon

fishhook

sock

hockey stick

Art by Rich Powell

How Much Rain?

horseshoe

crown

slice of
watermelon

canoe

needle

banana

sailboat

drinking straw

carrot

book

cat

broccoli

mitten

domino

high-heeled
shoe

asparagus

slice of pizza

Art by Brian Michael Weaver

84

Look at Them Grow!

sailboat

button

pencil

ice-cream cone

heart

baseball cap

muffin

glove

envelope

scissors

bell

sea star

teacup

toothbrush

banana

fish

fishhook

musical note

ruler

crown

closed umbrella

ring

needle

Art by Laura Freeman

Science Class

bell

tack

slice of pizza

star

sneaker

toothbrush

artist's brush

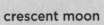

banana

crescent moon

hammer

fish

teacup

Art by Jackie Stafford

86

Beach Observations

bath brush

banana

bell

sock

crescent moon

open book

teddy bear

saw

leaf

dinosaur

strawberry

button

ladle

muffin

hat

Art by Laura Freeman

87

Snowshoe Scientists

banana

piece of
popcorn

butterfly

crown

clothespin

fishhook

jellyfish

sock

jump rope

drinking
straw

paper
airplane

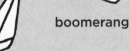

sailboat

boomerang

pencil

needle

toothbrush

wedge of lemon

wishbone

yo-yo

coat hanger

fish

necktie

open book

muffin

heart

fork

fried egg

candy corn

spool of thread

teacup

tack

Art by Laura Close

89

Dinosaur Museum

banana

drinking straw

kite

baseball bat

egg

wrench

candy cane

snowman

leaf

ice-cream cone

pencil

key

heart

snake

puzzle piece

ruler

toothbrush

slice of pizza

ice-cream bar

flag

comb

Art by Jennifer Harney

90

Science Fair Creations

pennant

bowl

flowerpot

ice-cream bar

golf club

slice of pie

kite

button

spool of thread

mug

banana

sock

candle

sailboat

snake

Bayou Biology

carrot

flag

jump rope

matchstick

sailboat

arrow

spoon

ruler

heart

scissors

lollipop

needle

kite

pear

broccoli

funnel

high-heeled shoe

open book

hot dog

green bean

saucepan

Art by Laura Close

92

Wind and Waves

Art by Sally Springer

slice of pizza

needle

heart

question mark

flag

toothbrush

tack

crescent moon

pencil

fishhook

ice-cream cone

musical note

shovel

pennant

Telescope Time

stamp

saltshaker

peanut

envelope

paper clip

comb

fried egg

artist's brush

spool of thread

toothbrush

flashlight

test tube

strawberry

slice of bread

drinking straw

game piece

ruler

Art by Dana Regan

94

Robot Building

toothbrush

mug

bell

bird

fishhook

nail

tack

crown

crescent moon

comb

lollipop

drinking straw

ring

pencil

Art by R. Michael Palan

95

A Whale of a Time

candle

ice-cream
cone

ruler

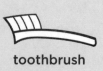

toothbrush

crescent
moon

nail

pencil

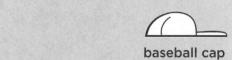

baseball cap

96

golf club

needle

banana

can

mug

pumpkin

sunglasses

heart

Art by Mike DeSantis

97

Feeding Fish

mushroom

dog bone

tennis racket

teapot

cookie

snail

cowboy hat

doughnut

pear

mitten

feather

drinking straw

ruler

slice of watermelon

baseball bat

mug

canoe

truck

pine tree

magnifying glass

sock

comb

bat

Art by Merrie Gallagher-Cole

98

Science Rules!

wristwatch

banana

comb

artist's brush

ring

slice of pizza

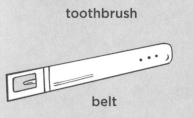
toothbrush

adhesive bandage

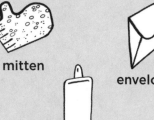
mitten

envelope

sailboat

belt

arrow

tack

bottle of glue

button

Art by Susan Miller

99

Hi There, Heron!

mitten

candle

toucan

toothpaste

slice of cake

banana

carrot

artist's brush

paper airplane

shoe

bell

umbrella

lollipop

toothbrush

spoon

balloon

soccer ball

eyeglasses

Art by Chuck Dillon

Rock Candy Crystals

ice-cream cone

shoe

wishbone

briefcase

chili pepper

question mark

slice of pizza

baseball bat

slice of pie

teakettle

egg

pennant

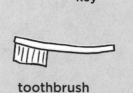
toothbrush

key

slice of bread

Art by Mary Sullivan

101

Deep-Sea Submarine

tack

candy corn

star

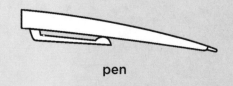
pen

nail

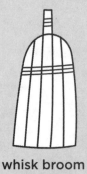
whisk broom

cookie

olive

mushroom

flag

crayon

wedge of cheese

Microscopic Marvels

Art by Dave Klug

pineapple

spool of thread

safety pin

ice skate

banana

bird

umbrella

kite

mouse

eyeglasses

butterfly

fish

sock

bell

mushroom

horseshoe

snail

hat

104

Geology Rocks

funnel

recorder

chili pepper

hourglass

boomerang

paintbrush

drinking straw

spool of thread

key

glove

button

toothbrush

mushroom

hedgehog

lightning bolt

snake

Art by Christine Schneider

Exploring the Lake

chili pepper

tooth

fried egg

musical note

spoon

crown

flag

closed umbrella

banana

nail

belt

candy cane

key

flashlight

ice-cream cone

Art by Scot Ritchie

Low-Gravity Games

baseball glove

spool of thread

rowboat

baseball cap

party hat

canoe

pennant

ring

slice of watermelon

seashell

mushroom

crown

tack

worm

flower

open book

leaf

ice skate

mug

107

Computer Lab

flashlight

drinking straw

lock

pencil

shovel

artist's brush

piece of popcorn

rake

scissors

heart

paper clip

needle

button

mushroom

ruler

sea star

pen

doughnut

crescent moon

spatula

postage stamp

adhesive bandage

broom

screwdriver

ice-cream bar

slice of watermelon

bell

envelope

caterpillar

leaf

lollipop

nail

fishhook

comb

teacup

domino

Art by Ellen Appleby

109

Collecting Samples

butterfly

flowerpot

number three

feather

teacup

baseball glove

open book

adhesive bandage

paintbrush

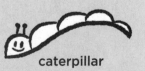
caterpillar

gingerbread cookie

crown

spoon

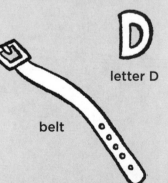
belt

letter D

Art by Joey Ellis

110

Careful Assembly Required

ruler

comb

worm

acorn

hamburger

magnet

lollipop

ladder

envelope

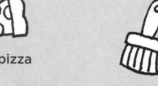
slice of pizza

paintbrush

wedge of orange

saltshaker

pencil

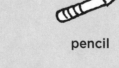
candy cane

Art by Patrick Girouard

111

Family Zoo Day

medal

ruler

banana

carrot

teacup

lightning bolt

toothbrush

jump rope

crown

slice of pizza

sock

hair dryer

whale

112

arrow

open book

slice of bread

candy corn

fork

heart

wishbone

necktie

pencil

nail

funnel

sailboat

spoon

potato

scissors

Art by Laura Close

113

Space Dreams

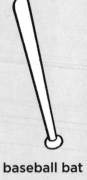
baseball bat

drumstick

ice-cream cone

envelope

paintbrush

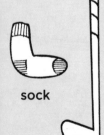
sock

golf club

114

pencil

saltshaker

crown

bow tie

bat

tack

sailboat

slice of pie

paper clip

Art by David Helton

Nature Center Visit

banana

necktie

golf club

ring

ice-cream bar

sailboat

crayon

fork

pencil

pail

football

bell

green bean

candy corn

arrow

sock

flowerpot

Art by Laura Close

Terrific Tyrannosaur

flowerpot

sailboat

game piece

wrench

candy cane

fish

elephant

light bulb

seashell

croissant

yo-yo

clothespin

scuba tank

paddle

umbrella

bug

teapot

pitcher

guitar

pillow

Art by Iryna Bodnaruk

Soundwaves in the Sky

open book

canoe

glove

waffle

cat's face

sailboat

heart

banana

118

shorts

piece of popcorn

ruler

carrot

pennant

dinosaur

crescent moon

golf club

slice of pizza

Art by Kevin Zimmer

Who's in the Tide Pool?

car

hockey stick

shoe

toaster

sock

grapes

feather

glove

banana

loaf of bread

rhino

eyeglasses

Art by Dave Klug

Observant Eyes

ice-cream bar

golf club

artist's brush

teacup

tent

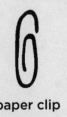
paper clip

ring

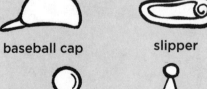
baseball cap

slipper

fish

lightning bolt

lollipop

party hat

bird

peapod

banana

120

Water Cycle Workshop

doughnut

ring

candle

spool of thread

mushroom

knitted hat

umbrella

bird

party hat

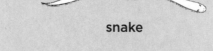
snake

carrot

toothbrush

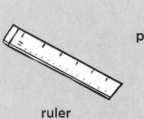
ruler

mug

light bulb

Art by Susan Miller

Immersive Oceanography

Art by Ellen Appleby

kite

worm

flower

carrot

lollipop

snake

button

artist's brush

fried egg

ghost

crescent moon

heart

comb

pliers

slice of watermelon

envelope

Hey, Comet!

football

potted plant

crown

teacup

pencil

paint can

fish

ring

slice of bread

triangle ruler

domino

lollipop

artist's brush

slice of watermelon

open book

wedge of lemon

heart

slice of pizza

Art by Hector Borlasca

Defying Gravity

cane

bow tie

heart

ice pop

hammer

hanger

envelope

carrot

musical note

baby's bottle

drumstick

boot

peanut

dustpan

banana

Art by Christine Schneider

124

Topographic Trek

 bird

surfboard

★ star

light bulb

shark

key

slice of pizza

sailboat

teacup

cloud

number
four

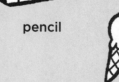
magnifying glass

pencil

ice-cream cone

rocket ship

Art by Joey Ellis

125

Community Garden

teacup

wedge of cheese

crown

crescent moon

elf's shoe

envelope

fish

glove

knitted hat

gingerbread cookie

game piece

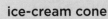
ice-cream cone

126

tent

heart

banana

musical note

snowman

ruler

lollipop

drinking straw

lightning bolt

muffin

paintbrush

Art by Laura Close

127

Objects in Motion

lemon

teacup

needle

lollipop

musical note

envelope

flag

golf tee

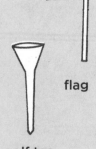
wishbone

heart

boot

scissors

baby's bottle

glove

radish

vase

sea star

traffic cone

128

Art by Gary Mohrmanv

Build-Your-Own Catapult

puzzle piece

snowman

comb

saucepan

mitten

carrot

fish

sock

canoe

crown

paper clip

umbrella

baseball bat

hammer

heart

toothbrush

spatula

shoe

golf club

Art by Dave Klug

129

Answers

▼ Pages 4–5

▼ Page 6

▼ Page 7

▼ Page 8

▼ Page 9

▼ Page 10

▼ Page 11

Answers

▼ **Pages 12–13**

▼ **Page 14**

▼ **Page 15**

▼ **Page 16**

▼ **Page 17**

▼ **Page 18**

▼ **Page 19**

▼ **Page 20**

Answers

▼Page 21

▼Page 22

▼Page 23

▼Pages 24–25

▼Page 26

▼Page 27

▼Page 28

▼Page 29

Answers

▼Page 30

▼Page 31

▼Pages 32–33

▼Page 34

▼Page 35

▼Page 36

▼Page 37

Answers

▼ Pages 38–39

▼ Page 40

▼ Page 41

▼ Pages 42–43

▼ Page 44

▼ Page 45

▼ Page 46

Answers

▼ Page 47

▼ Pages 48-49

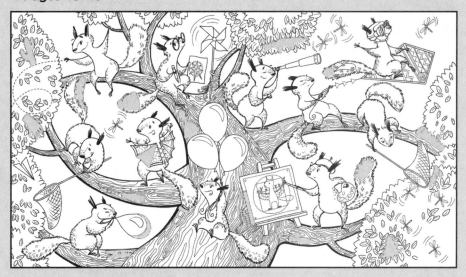

▼ Page 50

▼ Page 51

▼ Page 52

▼ Page 53

▼ Pages 54-55

Answers

▼Page 56

▼Page 57

▼Page 58

▼Page 59

▼Pages 60–61

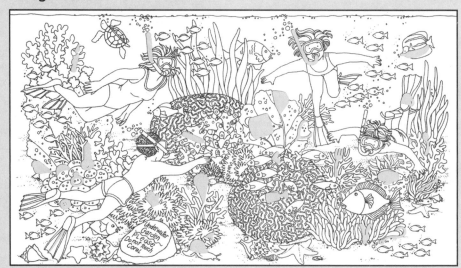

▼Page 62

▼Page 63

▼Page 64

Answers

▼Page 65

▼Pages 66–67

▼Page 68

▼Page 69

▼Page 70

▼Page 71

▼Page 72

▼Page 73

Answers

▼ Pages 74–75

▼ Page 76

▼ Page 77

▼ Page 78

▼ Page 79

▼ Page 80

▼ Page 81

Answers

▼ Pages 82–83

▼ Page 84

▼ Page 85

▼ Page 86

▼ Page 87

▼ Pages 88–89

▼ Page 90

Answers

▼Page 91

▼Page 92

▼Page 93

▼Page 94

▼Page 95

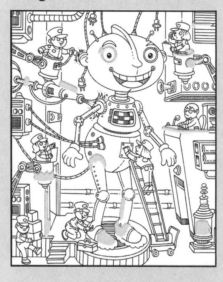

▼Pages 96–97

▼Page 98

Answers

▼ Page 99

▼ Page 100

▼ Page 101

▼ Pages 102–103

▼ Page 104

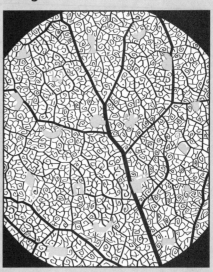

▼ Page 105

▼ Page 106

▼ Page 107

Answers

▼ Pages 108–109

▼ Page 110

▼ Page 111

▼ Pages 112–113

▼ Page 114

▼ Page 115

Answers

▼ Pages 116–117

▼ Page 118

▼ Page 119

▼ Page 120

▼ Page 121

▼ Page 122

▼ Page 123

▼ Page 124

Answers

▼Page 125

▼Pages 126–127

▼Page 128

▼Page 129

For information about permission to reprint
selections from this book, please contact
permissions@highlights.com.

Published by Highlights Press
815 Church Street, Honesdale, Pennsylvania 18431
ISBN: 978-1-64472-941-0
Manufactured in Robbinsville, NJ, USA
Mfg. 11/2022

First edition
Visit our website at Highlights.com.
10 9 8 7 6 5 4 3 2 1